MARIE ANTOINETTE
"MADAME DEFICIT"

By Liz Hockinson | Illustrated by Peter Malone

goosebottombooks

© 2011 Goosebottom Books LLC

Series editor **Shirin Yim Bridges**
Editor **Amy Novesky**
Copy editor **Jennifer Fry**
Editorial assistant **Ann Edwards**
Book design **Jay Mladjenovic**

Typeset in Trajan, Ringbearer, Volkswagen, and Gill Sans
Illustrations rendered in gouache

Manufactured in Singapore

Library of Congress Control Number: 2011924356

ISBN: 978-0-9834256-4-9

First Edition 10 9 8 7 6 5 4 3 2 1

Goosebottom Books LLC
710 Portofino Lane, Foster City, CA 94404

www.goosebottombooks.com

The Thinking Girl's Treasury of Dastardly Dames

CLEOPATRA
"SERPENT OF THE NILE"

AGRIPPINA
"ATROCIOUS AND FEROCIOUS"

MARY TUDOR
"BLOODY MARY"

CATHERINE DE' MEDICI
"THE BLACK QUEEN"

MARIE ANTOINETTE
"MADAME DEFICIT"

CIXI
"THE DRAGON EMPRESS"

To Amy, a most benevolent writing coach and friend. ~ **Liz Hockinson**

"Madame Deficit"

One spring morning, a pretty girl stepped into a horse-drawn carriage for the long journey from Austria to France. As the wheels bounced over rough roads, Marie Antoinette gazed at the portrait of the future king Louis XVI, in her hands. The prospect of marriage to the heir to the French throne made her giddy. One day she would become queen of one of the most powerful countries in Europe. But unlike her mother, the Empress Maria Theresa, who'd orchestrated this political marriage, Marie had no interest in politics, or in the real world outside the palace. What excited her about one day becoming queen was her vision of a grand life. And grand it would be. While her people starved, Marie Antoinette would live decadently and become infamous for supposedly uttering four little words: "Let them eat cake."

Where she lived

Paris, France's capital city, where Marie was executed.

Vienna, where Marie was born.

Versailles, home of the French court.

France

Austria

After she became queen, Marie lived in Versailles, the largest palace in Europe, just outside of Paris. During Marie's reign, Versailles housed 5,000 people and 2,000 horses. Except for the royal apartments, the rooms were small, dirty, and smelly; chamber pots were employed and emptied out of the nearest window.

When she lived

This timeline shows when the Dastardly Dames were born.

69 BC	15 AD	1516 AD	1519 AD	1755 AD	1835 AD
Cleopatra	Agrippina	Mary Tudor	Catherine de' Medici	Marie Antoinette	Cixi

Her Story

Marie Antoinette was born on November 2, 1755, in Vienna, Austria. She was the fifteenth of sixteen children born to Francis Stephen I and Maria Theresa, emperor and empress of the Holy Roman empire. Marie's family was one of the most important royal families of Europe in the middle of the eighteenth century.

Marie was a pretty child. Straw-colored hair complemented a porcelain complexion and delicately pink cheeks. But crooked teeth and an uneven hairline were not ideal, and she'd inherited a protruding lower lip, giving her a pouty, disdainful look that did not reflect the lighthearted young lady she actually was, nor would it do her future reputation any favors.

Marie's childhood home was the 1,400-room Schönbrunn Palace in Vienna, Austria. Today, the palace is open to the public and attracts more than two million visitors every year.

Marie's childhood was like a fairytale. She lived in a palace and she was spoiled beyond imagination, her every desire fulfilled by the royal staff. On warm days, she took walks in the palace gardens, played dolls with her sisters, and raced with her brothers, her beloved dogs nipping at her heels. In the winter, she loved sleigh rides and playing the harpsichord.

While Marie pursued artistic endeavors such as music and dance, intellectual standards for eighteenth-century princesses were not very high, and Marie was not well-educated. She could not read or write very well; she was nearly illiterate. And she had trouble concentrating, which was often mistaken for capriciousness.

Nonetheless, Marie's mother had high ambitions for her daughter. The Austrian empress sought to arrange royal marriages for all eleven of her daughters that would create fortuitous alliances for Austria. For her youngest daughter, Marie Antoinette, she had her eyes set on France. Austria and France had been enemies for almost 200 years.

Marie Antoinette was just fourteen years old when she was sent to France to marry the fifteen-year-old Dauphin, or heir to the throne, Louis Auguste. Marie had no idea that she would never see Austria again. At the Rhine River she was transferred to the Ile des Epis, an island considered neutral territory between France and Austria. In a small pavilion, every stitch of Marie Antoinette's clothing was removed and replaced with French royal fashions. Deeds were signed, a door opened, and Marie reluctantly walked away from everything she had ever known—when she looked back, her Austrian friends were gone. It is said that thunder rumbled in the nearby Black Forest during the ceremony and that Marie wept bitterly.

On May 16, 1770, Marie and Louis Auguste were married in the royal chapel at the Palace of Versailles. A young gawky groom, heavyset and slightly stooped, Louis was not the prince charming Marie might have hoped for. Myopia made him appear glum and disinterested, but after all he was just a teenager, too. That night, the future king and his bride were escorted to the marital chamber by the king himself, who helped dress them in their royal nightgowns and kissed them both good night. Marie's duty was to bear children, preferably a son, and secure the royal line. But not much happened that first night between the two teens, who'd met each other just days before. And not much happened the next night, or the night after that, or for years to come.

The newspapers of the day—like our tabloids in more recent times—were full of stories and pictures of the royal wedding.

You can still peek into the Royal Chapel at Versailles, and imagine Marie and Louis standing in front of its golden altar.

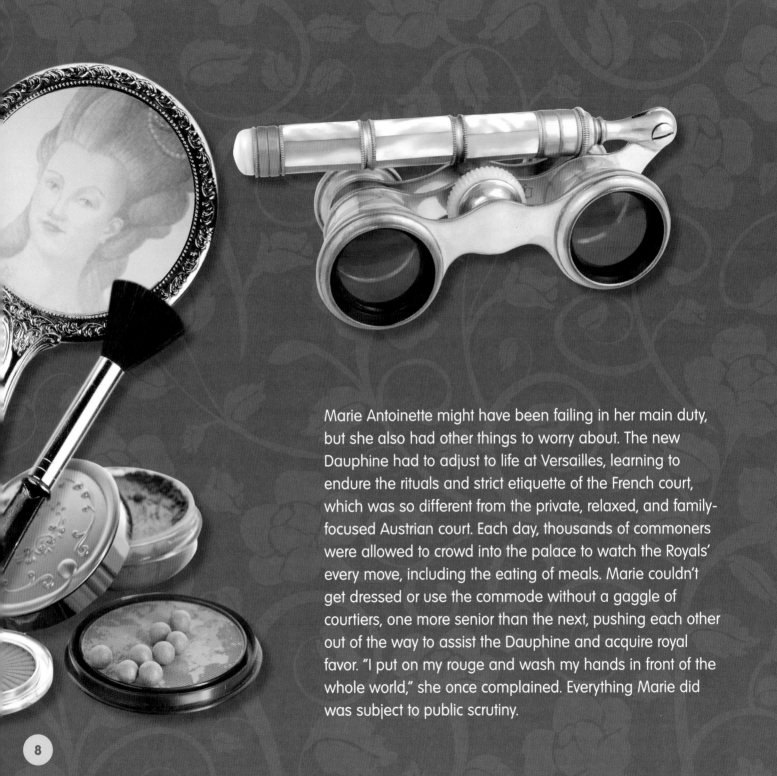

Marie Antoinette might have been failing in her main duty, but she also had other things to worry about. The new Dauphine had to adjust to life at Versailles, learning to endure the rituals and strict etiquette of the French court, which was so different from the private, relaxed, and family-focused Austrian court. Each day, thousands of commoners were allowed to crowd into the palace to watch the Royals' every move, including the eating of meals. Marie couldn't get dressed or use the commode without a gaggle of courtiers, one more senior than the next, pushing each other out of the way to assist the Dauphine and acquire royal favor. "I put on my rouge and wash my hands in front of the whole world," she once complained. Everything Marie did was subject to public scrutiny.

What she ate

The French court ate well and drank wine with every meal. The Austrians were more frugal and had simpler tastes. A typical meal at Versailles would consist of onion or potato soup, followed by sixteen entrée selections, including meats such as filet mignon, pheasant, veal, and roast beef, and vegetables such as artichokes, green beans, spinach, and mixed ragout. A vast array of rich confections and fancy pastries was offered for dessert.

Marie Antoinette ate small portions and foods that were not rich. Breakfast consisted of coffee or chocolate and croissants or little dipping biscuits; supper was soup with white meat of chicken.

The croissant. French, right? The croissant actually originated in Austria, created by Viennese bakers to celebrate a victory against the Turks. The croissant resembled the crescent, the symbol of Islam, featured on the Turkish flag. They became popular in Vienna and then, because of Marie's love for them, in France.

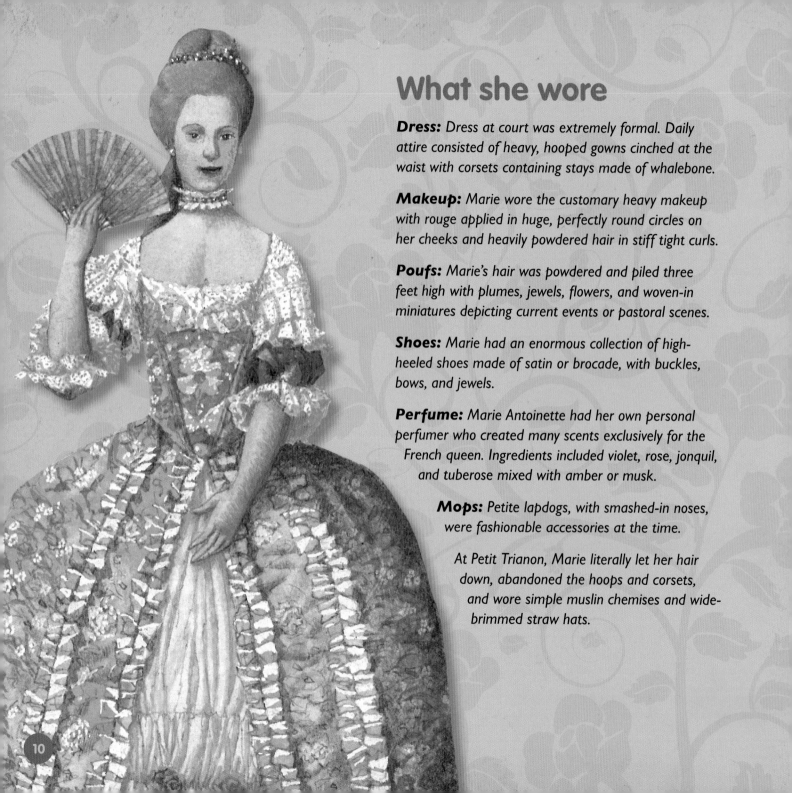

What she wore

Dress: *Dress at court was extremely formal. Daily attire consisted of heavy, hooped gowns cinched at the waist with corsets containing stays made of whalebone.*

Makeup: *Marie wore the customary heavy makeup with rouge applied in huge, perfectly round circles on her cheeks and heavily powdered hair in stiff tight curls.*

Poufs: *Marie's hair was powdered and piled three feet high with plumes, jewels, flowers, and woven-in miniatures depicting current events or pastoral scenes.*

Shoes: *Marie had an enormous collection of high-heeled shoes made of satin or brocade, with buckles, bows, and jewels.*

Perfume: *Marie Antoinette had her own personal perfumer who created many scents exclusively for the French queen. Ingredients included violet, rose, jonquil, and tuberose mixed with amber or musk.*

Mops: *Petite lapdogs, with smashed-in noses, were fashionable accessories at the time.*

At Petit Trianon, Marie literally let her hair down, abandoned the hoops and corsets, and wore simple muslin chemises and wide-brimmed straw hats.

This included Marie and Louis' private life. Doctors were sent in to check the couple. Everything seemed to be in working order. Louis just had no interest in being intimate with Marie Antoinette, and this was humiliating and devastating. As if that wasn't enough, Marie's mother kept chiding her, asking her if she was with child yet, imploring her to bear an heir and establish security for Austria. Marie's sisters were having babies, and so were Louis' brothers' wives, sparking a tense race to see who could produce the next male heir to the French throne. Marie's position was tenuous. If her marriage wasn't consummated it could be annulled by the Catholic Church. She felt like a failure.

Marie Antoinette is often credited (or blamed) for creating the extravagant fashions of her time, including looming hair pieces and skirts so wide that ladies had to enter a room sideways. However, in private, she often preferred to slip into something more comfortable. But when she was painted in her comfy clothes (above), there was an uproar. This was no way for a queen of France to be seen! The portrait had to be repainted (below).

And then, King Louis XV contracted smallpox and died within weeks. Louis and Marie fell to their knees and prayed to God for guidance; they felt too young to rule. The people, however, looked toward the new king and his glamorous queen in hopeful anticipation. After Louis XVI was crowned king, jubilant crowds filled the streets, church bells rang, and volleys of artillery filled the sky. Marie Antoinette was thrilled with their popularity. According to a French historian at the time, "She as yet knew nothing of the crown but its flowers." Soon, she would come to know the crown's full weight.

This is an artist's depiction of the original Crown of Charlemagne—used for centuries in the coronations of the French kings. It was destroyed during the French Revolution. Napoleon stole its name for a crown he had made to crown himself Emperor of France. You can see this more modern "Crown of Charlemagne" in the Louvre Museum.

This is a detail of a painting of Marie in her coronation robes, painted in 1775, by Jean-Baptiste Gautier Dagot. She was at the height of her popularity at the time, and as the painting suggests, it appeared as if the whole world was at her fingertips.

"Let them eat cake."

Most historians have concluded that Marie Antoinette never uttered these infamous words. "Qu'ils mangent de la brioche," was originally attributed to a Spanish princess who married Louis XIV a hundred years earlier, and it had been attached to other princesses since. Given Marie's notorious excess, the words fit perfectly into her mouth when they were put there, but they have since become something of a myth.

The royal celebration was in stark contrast to the realities the country faced. France was bleeding money, funding the American Revolution against England. The deficit was growing and the government faced bankruptcy. The tax system was extremely unfair, heavily burdening the working class, while aristocrats lived large and tax-free. A disastrous harvest, compounded by skyrocketing prices for wheat and flour, led to a shortage of bread. People were desperate and dying of starvation. This was followed by a winter so severe that the River Seine froze over. People had no heat, no food, and no hope. Marie Antoinette, still riding high from the recent coronation, was said to have dismissed the problem with, "Let them eat cake."

The truth is, Marie had no interest in politics, and there was no official role for her. The king did not include her in his governing, and she didn't really try to influence him, despite pressure from Austria to do so. Furthermore, she never saw, nor cared to see, how ordinary French people lived. Her world revolved around the court. And she indulged in court life.

Marie loved fashion, and as queen of the most fashionable country in the world, she lived up to her role as a trendsetter. Everyone in Paris wanted to dress like the queen. Wide-hooped gowns dusted with diamonds and gems exposed her ankles and made her modest cleavage blossom. It is said that she never wore a gown twice. Piled into three-foot-high poufs, her hair was heavily powdered and adorned (ironically) with pastoral scenes, and her pale cheeks flushed deeply with huge perfect circles of rouge.

Newspapers and magazines carried pictures of the queen's latest fashions. These would immediately be copied by dressmakers across the nation.

Dessiné par La Clere

Habit de Cour de satin Cerise, le ruban de tête de même, le coin de gaze
diamants, perles et ruban du tour de gorge blancs, ainsi que les glands du manteau
dans certaine partie sur la teinte du fond, le fond du fauteuil violet, et les armes selon
le tapis de pied de toutes couleurs.

Marie spent her nights at the theater, the opera, and masked balls dancing until dawn. She gambled at cards for days and lost fortunes. She rode a small gray donkey around the palace grounds and spent hours pampering her beloved pug dog, Mops. She acquired and decorated palaces, including her very own, Petit Trianon, which became known as her "pleasure house." There, she had a fake country village built, complete with a farmhouse, dairy, and mill, so that she and her ladies could play at being milkmaids, using porcelain milk churns specially made by the royal porcelain factory and painted to look as if they were made from wood. She flirted with handsome princes, inviting accusations of dalliances. She loved to laugh. And the French believed that great queens did not laugh.

The Petit Trianon, a small chateau on the grounds of the Palace of Versailles. This private chateau had been built for the mistresses of Louis XIV and Louis XV and then given to Marie for her exclusive use. No one was permitted to enter the property except by order of the queen.

The Hameau, or model village, at the Petit Trianon. Marie's idyllic hamlet consisted of twelve cottages, a hermitage, a belvedere, allegorical temples consecrated for love and friendship, dovecotes, an aviary, a henhouse, and a dairy, complete with cows. Over 1,000 white porcelain pots inscribed with the queen's blue monogram were filled with flowers, and the grounds were lush with jasmine, rose, myrtle, lilacs, and fluttering butterflies.

This portrait of the queen and her children by
Élisabeth Vigée-LeBrun celebrates Marie's eventual
success at providing France with royal heirs.

Marie was frivolous and uneducated. She was Austrian, and the French hated the Austrians. They called Marie, "l'Autrichienne" or "the Austrian woman." But they were also calling her a dog, or bitch, as the name contains the French word for a female dog, "chienne." Marie wouldn't have known, as her French was horrendous.

The question on everyone's mind was: would this pampered and impulsive woman ever give birth to an heir? Finally, after seven years of marriage, the queen did her duty. As was the custom in the court, Marie delivered her baby in front of hundreds. The airless room was so crowded that when Marie passed out amid the press of spectators, no one noticed. Everyone was disappointed that the baby, Marie Therese, was merely a girl. Then the baby's paternity was questioned; after all, it was well known that the king and queen rarely shared a bed. Still, the baby was blessed, money was thrown to the crowd by the handfuls, and wine flowed in the fountains.

The baby girl was followed by a boy, Louis Joseph. But the frail heir to the throne would die of consumption eight years later, and a second daughter, Sophie Beatrix, would not see her first birthday. A second son, Louis Charles, survived to be the new Dauphin. Marie was devoted to her children, and motherhood and maternal loss mellowed her. She partied less and dressed more conservatively. She literally let her hair down, wiped the rouge from her cheeks, and, when in private, wore simple muslin dresses and wide-brimmed hats. But by then the image of Marie as an extravagant queen was indelible.

The pencil sketch above was made by a spectator while the queen was actually in labor! Below, another of Marie's bedrooms, this one in the Chateau de Fontainebleau.

Her own courtiers were calling her Madame Deficit—she was so careless and so extravagant she was blamed for bankrupting the country. The people could see that their beloved queen didn't care about them at all. This growing fervor was fueled by libelles—the tabloids of the day—which portrayed the queen as wicked and the king as weak. She was called careless, vicious, adulterous, perverse, even murderous. Some believed she intended to poison the king, and these caricatures were so often repeated in papers that sold like hotcakes that surely, they had to be true. Once loved by all, Marie Antoinette was now hated—so hated, she was hissed at.

Le Promenoir Royal ou La fuite er

The media played a large role in the French Revolution. Pamphleteers made fun of the king and queen, and both expressed and fueled the frustrations of a nation. Later, they documented the atrocities of the killing spree that became known as the Reign of Terror.

The queen's unpopularity and the king's ineffectiveness undermined the monarchy. Paris rioted. The people demanded more rights. A mob stormed the Bastille in search of weapons. (They even raided the opera house but were disappointed to discover that the props were made of cardboard). The people had no bread, but now they had guns and ammunition. They demanded an end to the monarchy. France was in revolution.

The revolutionaries imprisoned thousands of people. In the center of Paris, a new execution device called the guillotine was constructed. Over 15,000 people—royalty, nobility, and in the end, commoners alike—would lose their heads.

The guillotine

The inventor of the guillotine was Dr. Joseph Ignace Guillotin, a French physician and founder of the French Academy of Medicine. The guillotine's swiftness was thought to make the execution more humane. The executioner pulled a handle to release a huge blade that fell with the force of gravity to decapitate the victim. Over 15,000 heads rolled throughout France during the French Revolution.

Royalists fled France for fear of assassination. Marie Antoinette, whose life was in the most danger, stayed behind to be with the king. Soon enough, a mob composed mostly of women marched from Paris to Versailles to demand flour from the king. Wearing aprons, they vowed to cut off Marie Antoinette's head and make cockades, or ribbons, of her entrails. The king gave orders to release the royal granaries, but this did not appease the mob. Rioters broke into Marie Antoinette's chambers and hacked her bed to smithereens. The queen just managed to escape through a secret passageway. In the end, the mob escorted the king and queen back to Paris, brandishing sticks, picks, and axes, all the while singing a popular song, "The Baker's Wife."

The king and queen were put under house arrest at Tuileries Palace, and monitored by revolutionary spies. They tried to escape, dressed as servants, heading for the royalist stronghold of Montmédy on the Austrian border. But twenty-four hours into their escape, they were recognized and forced to return to Paris. Crowds jeered and booed them along the road, and some threatened to shoot the queen.

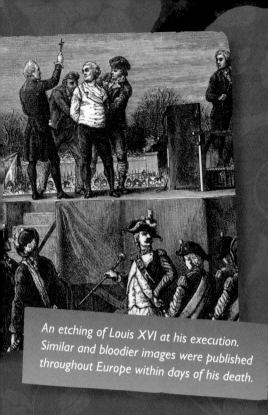

An etching of Louis XVI at his execution. Similar and bloodier images were published throughout Europe within days of his death.

Marie and Louis and their family were next imprisoned in the tower of the Temple of Marais, a 600-year-old fortress. The revolutionaries deposed the king. Now he was no more than a common man. Louis was brought to trial before the newly formed National Convention, found guilty of high treason, and condemned to death by the guillotine. The sound of drumbeats was followed by shouts of joy. Marie was grief-stricken. Until the day of her own death, she wore a simple black mourning dress. It was said that her hair turned white overnight.

And then the guards came for Marie's son. Despite her weakened state, Marie fought fiercely to keep him. It was no use. Louis XVII, the Little King, would die of abuse and tuberculosis two years later. Finally, Marie Antoinette faced her own trial. She was accused of depleting the national treasury, conspiring to ignite a civil war, and treason, among other things. She appealed to the mothers in the courtroom. Ironically, the market women who had marched against her now softened toward her. But the jury found her guilty of being an enemy of the state and sentenced her to be guillotined on the following day at noon.

Hours before she was to die, Marie wrote a letter to her sister-in-law. About being Madame Deficit, among other things, she claimed a clear conscience, despite conceding earlier at the trial, "Perhaps more was spent than I would have wished."

An illustration of Marie facing her accusers at the Revolutionary Tribunal. By all accounts she conducted herself with great dignity—and not like the frivolous princess she had once been. But it was not enough to save her. She was condemned to be executed the following day at noon.

A famous drawing of Marie on her way to execution, sketched by the painter Jacques-Louis David from his window as she passed by.

A tumbrel pulled by heavy horses carried Marie Antoinette slowly to the guillotine. She wore a simple white gown, her hair newly shorn, her hands bound in rope behind her back. She climbed the scaffold, accidentally stepping on her executioner's foot, for which she apologized. After the blade came down, her head was held up for all to see. It was 12:15 pm on Wednesday, October 16, 1793. Marie Antoinette, Madame Deficit, the Careless Queen, was buried in an unmarked grave.